Oh, Yes,

Yes, You Can!

Principles Of Leapology®

By

Matt Upton

Published

on

Ezekiel Noah's 2nd Birthday

October 30, 2018

Leap On

Practices of Leapology®

Gratitude for those that "In-Couraged" me to Leap

My Grandparents who always treated me as though I was what they believed I could be, rather than the person I was

My Mom and Dad who always loved me and did their very best to prepare me to Leap

For my three brothers who have inspired and given me "In-Couragement" to Leap on in spite of my failures, flops, and frustrations.

Rita Jo, for always believing I could make the Leap

For my Children who have live the principles and practices of Leapology®

For my Grandchildren who are the VP's of my world, you have taught me to Leap forward into the unknown, knowing that we are provided for, protected, and propelled forward

For each critic whose heart was against my Leap, for you may have been my most powerful teacher, professor, and trainer in the practices and principles of Leapology®. *I have left some mistakes, errors, and omissions just for you.*

I am ever so grateful for those of you who know the struggle and joy of living the Principles of Leapology®. It is my hope that my heart, my voice, my "In-Couragement" will come through each and every printed word and speak to you saying "Oh, Yes, Yes You Can!

Endorsements from Leapologist:

This book will inspire, motivate, and challenge the reader to leap from the place of normalcy and perceived security, to a greater place of purpose and satisfaction. Oh yes, yes you can.

Bishop Charles Ware, New Birth Christ Center

Matt's heartfelt, practical and positive approach to life is so inspiring! He encourages us to take the Leap and dig down deep into our souls to become the best person that we all know we can become. Matt walks us through the very real fears of life and uses "Leapology®" to give us the tools we need to achieve our best self. By taking responsibility for our lives, truly listening to others, being present and investing in one another, we can discover the unlimited possibilities waiting for us. "Navigate the possibilities rather than the problems". "Oh, Yes, Yes You Can!" is a must read for everyone navigating through life. Matt will be there to share in your journey. He is one of the most caring, compassionate people I know and am proud to call him my friend.

Bonnie Britt, Regional Sales Manager for S.A. Piazza &
Associates

Introduction:

Matthew has been a part of our family since he was a teenager. He was put through many tests while he was still young, and I saw him go through all these struggles still trusting God. Matthew has grown from each of these incidents to become an honorable and loyal man. I have always encouraged him to write a book because whatever it was that kept him going with the positive attitude and love he has, I knew we could all learn from it! He didn't have a name for it then, but he lived the principles that are in this book. It amazed me how he could be abused, maligned, stabbed in the back by people he loved and yet never return evil for evil. He did not even complain or feel sorry for himself when he was mistreated. It reminds me of the scripture that says, "you overcome evil with good." That's Matthew in a nutshell. This book gives us hope and some of the secrets that he has learned through his ups and downs.

Happy to take this Leap with him!

Joan Condit, Leader in Silent Strength Concepts

To leap into this book or not to Leap:

The following pages are here for those who are experiencing the call to the next location in their life. You stand in this space you've created and sense that there's more for you. You have grown weary of the relationship you have with your Now, this status que that has developed around you.

What they are also here for those who have come to the knowledge that though many of the events in your life you did not choose; yet you did decide on your response to them. You also recognize that due to your choices you are responsible for this space that surrounds you. You are the architect of your current Now. You've come to the edge of knowing there is no one, and no incident in and of itself, that is responsible for your perspective only you and your choices. So you have dispensed with blaming, and bought into rebuilding, through taking personal responsibility.

Together we will discover the principles of Leapology® and begin the thrilling work of building a life that is worth living. There will be times that we face fear down and advance in spite of its daunting voices telling us to play it safe.

Yes, it's true that those who play it safe come home safe, yet not many that play it safe have a life filled with adventure and trophies to mark their journey.

You have something within you that is calling you to the next space in your life. It is as if you sense a voice beckoning you to come over here and live again.

You've attempted to ignore it, to silence it, yet it breaks through your attempts to silence them and place them on the back shelf, far from your view and ability to hear them, It shows up in the music you listen to, it meanders across the movie screen as you watch the show. It lifts itself off the pages of articles and books you read. There are times as you connect with people outside your circle of family and friends that it speaks through their hearts voice.

If your presence is not described above, then the words and principles of Leapology® are not for you, you will be bored quickly through the following pages. Return this book and get your money back, or gift it to someone you believe is ready to make the Leap to the next plateau of their life. Life is too short to waste your time in reading something that's not for you.

If you are still here, then I want you to know that Oh, Yes, Yes you Can! You can and will make the Leap from here to the next place in your life's journey.

Welcome to your new Life of living by Leapology®

Leap On

Letting Go, to Go Forward

Chapter one

Thirty feet above the ground nestled in the redwoods of the Santa Cruz mountains, at Koinonia Conference Grounds, we gaze across the divide between two trees. In front of us are two ropes: one below that we are expected to walk on, and one above that has seven dangling ropes. Each rope has a large knot at its end. Each of us are harnessed into a safety harness which makes it impossible to fall to our severe injury or death.

As we cling to the large redwood tree, the facilitator gives us our task. "Each of you will walk from where you are now to the other tree. This will lead you to the next adventure of our course today", she states with an alarming sense of calm."

She further told us there's nothing to be afraid of, its safe and that many had gone before us, she then asked us "do you have any questions?". "How do we get from here to there without falling?" someone asked? Another exclaims "I do not think I can!" "Oh, Yes, Yes You Can" we heard back from the ground.

Each of us waited for someone else to go first. I am not sure why the others waited, yet I do know why I did. There were two reasons, I did not want to be the first one to attempt and fail; I was being harassed by fear. The other reason is I did not want to take away from someone who had the courage to go first and achieve the goal of moving from this tree we were hugging to the next tree; which would give access to the next adventurous obstacle.

Next thing I know is I am being "volun-told" that I am going first, out onto this rope that is about ¾" in diameter and 30 feet above the ground. Though I am wrapped in my safety harness and it has been tested so that I cannot plummet to the ground below, my mind forgot this in the midst of the fear that is challenging me to play it safe.

Looking back on that day I lived the first principle of Leapology® which is you have to "Let go, to Go forward".

Stepping from the plateau of safety onto the small redwood deck nestled near 30 feet above the ground, meant I had to, as an act of my will, listen to the facilitators encouraging words "Oh, Yes, Yes You Can!" and step out from the platform onto this small rope that moved as I placed my weight on it.

The ropes hanging down from the rope above were unreachable until I placed one of my feet completely on the tightrope below and lifted my other foot from the platform.

Experiencing life to its fullest involves Letting go and taking risk to go forward. What is stopping you from leaping from here towards your life that's worth living?

That day in the Santa Cruz Mountains 30 feet above the ground at Koinonia Conference Grounds all seven of us made it across that great divide. Some of us have a life long bond to that moment that will remain with forever.

Each dangling rope was just beyond my reach, which demanded that I let go of the safety and security of the rope in my hand, to grasp the next rope. After making it to the other side, there was still one of us was still trapped by fear. They were paralyzed by the unknown. Nothing we said could stifle the voice of fear that was paralyzing her. She had a vice-like grip on the tree where the rest of us had come from.

Making my way back to her across the tightrope, that had moments ago presented me with such fear and conjured up all my inabilities, now was not an obstacle because someone I cared for was stranded and truly wanted to move forward.

Once I made it to her, I wrapped my courage around her and whispered in her ear "Oh, yes, Yes You Can!". We breathed deep and moments later stepped from the safety of our former plateau and began our journey to our new place of safety.

Once she let go and began moving forward she never looked back. There were moments that challenged us along the journey, yet both of us wanted the new platform more than the one we just left behind.

The first principle of Leapology® is that you must want what's ahead more than what you currently have. Nothing and no one can coach you from the plateau of safety you are on. It is your own choice to let go and go forward or not. If someone or something other than yourself forces you to let go and go forward, you will look back and possibly desire to return.

Once you let go of this plateau of safety you will encounter hardships, obstacles, and crises of courage.

While 30 feet above the earth and in our safety harnesses, there was no way to get hurt. Yet, we had to constantly remind ourselves of this fact.

In our life's journey we are provided for, protected, and watched over as we leap. The Creator of the universe has our best interest at heart. The Source of all things is like that safety harness we had wrapped around us that day in the trees. It would not allow us to plummet to the earth nor could we get hurt.

You and I are just as safe as we leap towards our best selves and our fulfillment.

Once each of us arrived safely across the chasm, we celebrated and congratulated each other for conquering that taunting voice of fear. Though all of us celebrated not all of us went to the next obstacle.

There are seven elements to the first principle of Leapology®

1st **Current** adversity is often a gift to us, because it is proving to us that we are safe as we adventure forward.

.

2nd Accepting and living in the knowledge that we are provided for, protected, and propelled forward as we journey to be our best selves and experience fulfillment.

New!.

How to control

3rd Staying where you are now, is okay, as long as you stay because you have no sense of call to the next plateau. Allow no one and nothing to move you, except when you sense that you must leap.

4th Trials and Tribulations are part of the journey. Embrace them, celebrate their gift to you. They come to give you confidence in your abilities and your heart.

5th Investigating the possibility of moving forward has the capacity of igniting something within you that will result in a new life.

6th Negotiating the obstacles to your new plateau will produce courage and confidence for the other obstacles in your future.

7th **Gratitude is the illuminator of the steps** in front of you that are unseen, as you prepare to leap.

Oh, yes, Yes You Can! Yet you will never know that until you take the leap. If you can place the thought on the shelf and not think of it any longer, then stay where you are. However, if you cannot go long without glancing forward to that distant location, that distant relationship, or that distant career, then you must strap on your safety harness and climb the tree as we did that day. Breathe in the air of pressing forward and allow it to energize you to look forward.

It will take faith, courage, and doing to leap forward. It may be time to stop talking about what needs to be done and just begin doing.

The knowledge of how will be known as you leap. The provision will be delivered as you let go and move towards the ledge. The scrapes and bruises you receive in the process will serve as your teachers, trainers, and professors.

Enjoy the journey, now Let Go, and move forward.

Oh, Yes, Yes You Can!

An exercise to build your stamina to make the forward leap. Write down the following words and read them aloud at least three times a day over the next seven days.

Though I do not know
everything about my journey;
I do know that I am
Protected in the midst of
difficulty.
I know I am Provided for
while in pursuit of my
best self.
I know I am Watched over
in my journey.
I Leap in Faith because I
must
I Leap as a result of my own
choice to do so.

The reason I ask you to write this out is there is power in writing it out saying it our loud to yourself. Get your pen and paper now and begin to write. Once you have it in your handwriting, write it out two more times. Now that you have three handwritten copies, put each one in a different location that you will see at least three times throughout the next seven days. When you read them, read them out loud to yourself.

Your soul's stamina to stay the course will increase and the taunting voice of fear will get smaller. Let me know through email how this is helping you. Email me at Success@MattUpton.net and we will celebrate together the beginning of your living through Leapology®.

Remember "Oh, yes, Yes You Can!"

From Four Wheels to Two

Chapter two

Stepping out onto the porch in my black canvas tennis shoes, jean cutoffs and no shirt into the warm morning air of Anderson, California, I loved Saturday mornings because my Dad was home from work and I could spend time around him outside. As I stood there that spring morning, looking across the gravel road in front of our home, the cows seemed happy that it was the weekend as well. The air smelled good and the birds chirped as if they were singing about this remarkable morning.

Our home faced the south and it was an open yard with a huge tree in the middle. My brothers and I would attempt to climb up into

it, yet the trunk was too big for us to so.
Shorty, my dog lay next to it in the shade. He
was a small dog with medium length white,
and two-tone brown hair. Sometimes he
would sit up on his rear-end with his legs
dangling, looking for me. This morning was
like all the other Saturday mornings, except
for what my Dad was doing in the driveway
behind the car.

"Dad, what happened to my bike?" I asked as
I walked towards him. My Dad had my
Schwinn Stingray bicycle upside down and he
was using his tools on the back tire. Dad,
without even looking at me answered "today
son, you will ride with two wheels." "It's time
to grow up and ride with no training wheels."

In that moment the birds stopped singing,
the cows no longer smiled, and Shorty sat

down as fear took over my mind and heart
"No, NO I cannot, I am not ready" I quickly
responded. He just kept working away as if I
had said nothing.

The training wheels were laying on the drive
way and my Stingray rested on its kickstand.
"Come here son, it's time to grow up and ride
on two wheels" he demanded. Standing there
as he motioned for me to get over there, I
wanted to go back into the safety of the house
and my bedroom. Yet, I found myself slowly
moving towards him wondering how I was
going to get out of doing this. I knew I was
not ready and that I would most certainly get
hurt. Standing next to my Dad, I reminded
him that "No, No I cannot do this!"

"Oh, Yes, Yes you Can, and you will" he
stated as he reached out to grab my arm and

pull me close to my bicycle. I suppose he sensed my yearning to run and hide from this life changing moment. After several moments of a three-way conversation, one between me and myself, my dad and I, and this beast of fear within me. Dad lifted me and placed me on the banana seat and positioned on the gravel drive way pointing towards the end of the driveway.

Running behind me and my bike while I am saying out loud what I am both feeling and hearing inside of me, "Dad, I cannot do this." Dad's hand is on the back end of my seat and he is shouting his belief in that I can ride the bike. The taunting voice of fear muffled his voice of encouragement and faith in my abilities and turned his words into something completely different and opposite.

Dad, as always, wanted my best effort and believed in me and my potential for success. He knew that I could do this and that it was time to take the leap from the safety of four wheels to two on that gravel driveway.

Something odd happened that morning in the midst of my anxiety and fear. Dad's voice grew distant and not as loud. Now I was passing our neighbors driveway, while still loudly voicing my objections. Dads voice broke through the barrier of fear and anxiety and I thought I heard him say, "You're doing it Son, you're doing it". "Son, I told you Oh, Yes, Yes You Can".

In the spring of my second grade I was now riding my bicycle without the training wheels. Dad was right, he knew all along I could do this. Somewhere in the midst of passing the second house on our little gravel street, with my confidence growing; bam I went down on the gravel driveway!

Turning to my Dad, who was back in our driveway leaning against the back of the car, I yelled at him, "See, I told I can't do this, I am not ready!" The blood was running down my shins from both knees and small pieces of gravel in my elbows was the proof that I cannot do this.

Dad, finished his cigarette and did not respond to my outburst, just said, "Oh, Yes, Yes You Can, and you will get back on that bike and ride it again." Then he picked me up, brushed the gravel from my knees and elbows, placed me back on this torture device called a two-wheel bicycle and pointed me to the end of the driveway. "Now, ride son, ride" as he thrusted me down the road.

With dried blood on my shins and forearms I rode that Saturday morning and have been riding ever since Dad moved me from the safety of four wheels to two.

The second principle of Leapology® is that others may see and believe in your need to leap long before you do.

"Oh, Yes, Yes You Can!"

I learned six lessons on Leapology® that bright Saturday spring morning.

- **G**rabbing the handlebars with a sense of gratitude, even though in fear was a leap forward.

- **R**emembering that someone knows you can will give you courage

- **A**ccepting the challenge to move forward is where Leaping begins

- **V**alidating another's progress is powerful for both of you

- **E**levating someone to an opportunity can bring out their best

- **L**iberating others from their fear, through your belief in them, can free them to take the Leap

That day, taking the leap from four wheels to two, had a ripple effect on my brothers.

Though I had no idea it would. They learned to ride on two wheels much faster and with less injury that did. It seemed as though they had only confidence through their leap to two wheels.

Gaining a fulfilling life of adventure and advancement involves four other things that I experienced that cool Spring Saturday morning. In truth it has taken a life time to come to the point where I've learned the life lessons of that day.

That morning standing on the porch and realizing that because my Dad had decided it was time to ride on two wheels, the voice of fear filled my soul's ears and heart.

If given a choice I would have ran the other way, gone back to bed, volunteered to do housework, anything except get on that bike and crash and die. Sometimes you will not take the Leap and experience the gifts of Leapology® unless there's no way out. That day my "no way out" was my Dad making me do it, even to having to place me on the bike not just once, but twice.

What I had no concept of that day, was my brothers watching, and I believe secretly hoping I would make it back from the ride. Later, when it was their turn, it was easier because I had done it. Because you are a person of influence there are people viewing how you take your leaps and handle your gravel crashes. As you get up and dust yourself off, you create a ripple effect of courage. This wave of courage enables others to have success through your courage.

The pain of falling to the gravel and its grinding into my elbows and knees made me listen to my Dad. It also, made me keenly aware of, my own ability to sustain balance and to discover success.

Oh, Yes, Yes You Can!

With blood streaks that had now dried from the scrapes on both knees and elbows, I rode with a great sense of courage and pride to the end of the little gravel road we lived on. I rode with the wind, until I realized I did not know how to stop or turn this torture device! Even though it had become an exciting adventure.

At the end of the road was a barbed wired fence with a large blackberry bush through it. I had to quickly turn, stop, or crash into the blackberry bush. It had never crossed my mind that this would be an issue.

As I began the turn, bam I went down for my third time. More scrapes and bruises. This time though I did not need Dad to put me back on the bike, I got it up, dusted myself off and pointed it towards the house. Then off with the wind I rode back to the driveway where I had fearfully begun just 30 minutes or so ago.

It is through the eyes and heart of gratefulness I re-live that Saturday Spring morning, that I am able to watch that day on the monitor in my soul, I hear the birds singing, see the cows smiling, and Shorty cheering me on, and my Dad beaming with pride.

Choosing to view your journey as you leap from one plateau to the next plateau with gratefulness, recolors and reframes to bring out the best of each leap.

Reframing and Recoloring

Many of the events of our lives are horrible and unjust. They are laced with injustice and pain, yet we get to decide how to color and frame them.

The stories we paint in our hearts mind, and tell others, has the power to lift or land. They either can be told through the languish of the event, or the launching of it to a bigger and better life. The choice is ours.

Here are seven tools that can aid you in how you paint and frame your past.

1st Tool   Fix your heart on the fact that you are Provided for, Protected, and Projected towards your best life.

2nd Tool   Face the pain of it and forgive. Knowing that forgiveness is not granting a pardon to the person who treated you wrong. It is the setting yourself free from having to drink from the BAR of Bitterness, Anger, and Resentment.

3rd Tool	Find at least one thing about it that has created a good thing in your life and character; then talk about it with the quotation marks of gratefulness.
4th Tool	Follow the example of what you believe is the right thing to do. Be fully committed to do what is right regardless of the circumstances.
5th Tool	Fly what you learned through those events, knowing that they influence both you and those that listen to you.
6th Tool	Flip your vision from what they did wrong to you, to what you've gained through

it and your commitment to do what is correct.

7th Tool   Forfeit your right to languish in what happened and liberate yourself to live by the knowledge of tool #1

Take the Leap Right Now and send me a short email or text and share with me how this chapter has helped you; how it has given you courage to live through Leapology®

Email: Success@MattUpton.net

Phone Number: 916.708.8103

I look forward to hearing from you and getting to experience your Leaps with you.

Oh, Yes, Yes You Can!

Rest in Your Why

Chapter Three

Relaxing on the side of the roadway in the cool breeze of Judea's December weather, the young leader and his team observed men working in a farmer's field. This young leader with a growing influence as the evening of his time approached. He never used Facebook®, Twitter®, LinkedIn®, or any social media to gain a larger shadow of influence. Yet what caused his influence to grow to such magnitude?

His life was cut short at the age of 33, with only three years to accomplish his life's mission. He experienced raging character assaults from those in positions of leadership and power. Yet, those of commonality embraced and cherished him.

As the sun was resting in the west a debate broke out among those closest to him. "Ask me what you wish, what do you want", he asked after overhearing their debate. Two of the twelve members of his board of closest influencers wanted to secure a position of influence. It is likely that their Mom encouraged them to go after this elevated station.

The other ten perked up and paid close attention to his response to their inquiry. Probably while never taking his gaze from the field being cared for by the various men, He began his answer.

When you and I are being persuaded to move to the edge of our current comfort zone, with a sense that there's something more for us out beyond where we stand, we had better have the stamina to make the leap. Where does this endurance to continue come from? How can we ensure we have what it takes to go all the way?

As in the life of this young leader, all endeavors to the next space of our life come with the same four paradoxical conflicts.

1st Paradoxical Conflict

No one has ever done exactly what you have within you to do. Which means there's no one to show you the precise steps you must take to be successful.

With no one to get advice from, you will need to get out of your head and trust you heart and gut and begin. Yes, there are many that have launched out on their own journey, yet never on the one you are about to take, because it is yours and only yours.

Certainly, you can play it safe and stay in your current comfort zone. The problem is it is no longer inhabitable by you, you will only be happy in the next space. Your peace, your fulfillment is no longer available for you here; it is over there.

Take a look at your journey thus far, you've experienced other (probably many) situations just like this conflict of comfort. Yet, you leaped, lived and thrived. Now you are being called to take up residence over there on your new plateau.

Oh, yes, Yes You Can!

2nd Paradoxical Conflict

There will be a lack of friends and family lining up to encourage you to leap from your comfort zone to your next plateau. There are three reasons for them discouraging you, rather than "In-Couraging" you.

A. Their love for you will not allow them to be a part of you advancing into harm or failure. They mean well yet are blinded by love.

B. They find some of their livelihood through what you are currently doing. This causes them to desire for you to stay where you are, so they will continue to be taken care of. This is not only in a financial way, it can also be in an emotional way.

C. They have a similar calling to leap into their own bigger and better life and have decided to play it safe. They have backed away from the leap zone and anchored down. As a result, their only response to you is to discourage you from taking the Leap. Because if you do, they will need to do something else, as well.

Sometimes they will leap. Most of the time they will hurl rocks of accusations towards you. They will gossip about you, they will slander you, they will unfriend you. Though their attitude will be painful, they will serve as vitamins of courage as you Leap on.

3rd **Paradoxical Conflict**

There will be a lack of peace and confidence within you about the upcoming leap. This is caused by the first two paradoxical conflicts as well as one more.

Because no one has done what you are getting ready to do, the way you are getting ready to do it, you will look squarely into the unknown. You've never been there before, and if you are not careful, you will spend a lot of time in your head. Most of the time head trips cause you to travel toward, pain, predicaments, and plummeting. Staying is certainly easier and safer (in the short term), especially if you are not meant to leap. Yet, if you are meant to take the leap and remain here you will bring about much discomfort, anxiety, and burdens.

"G-Ma, just imagine, if ..." a friend of mines grandson often says to her. Our imagination can either serve as an anchor or the building materials to launch us. It is our choice.

4th **Paradoxical Conflict**

Often taking the leap involves leaving loved ones behind. They have not, nor can they experience what you are sensing within your soul. That calling, that luring, that compelling to the edge of the comfort zone and taking that leap to the next plateau of your life, is for you alone.

Your ability to influence them is in taking the leap with courage and confidence, not in staying. Yes, they will be emotional, maybe even express disappointment in your leaping, yet, your success will change their hearts from sadness to gladness and disappointment to making appoints with their own destinies through the Leap Zone.

While his team of men argued about who would be the greatest among them, the young leader never lost sight of his life's mission. Many of us get lost and travel down paths we were never meant to go down, because we attempt to win the "good opinions" of those around us, or we are seeking fame and fortune.

There is an intoxicating dilemma in both of these goals. Both have within them a hallucinogen, that will cause you to see, hear, and feel things that are not real nor good for you. It also has the capacity to cause you to accept less than your best. Then a person will seek the fix of "good opinions" more than the satisfaction of your life's mission. You will step on people, violate your high standard, and accept a life of just good enough, rather than a life energized through the power of Leapology®.

Knowing his own "Why" and staying firmly enveloped by it, kept him balanced and capable of maneuvering through everything in his life. He committed to their request "I have come to Serve, and not be served", and "those that would be the greatest among you, must become the least."

His life commitment to serve sustained him through peril, persecution, pressure, plots against him, plans to set him up to higher positions, and people with other plans for him. This helped him to become to greatest man to ever walk on earth.

Because of him the calendar changed, holidays were created, customs cultivated, and all this without ever tweeting, Facebooking, texting, video blogging, or any other source of social media. He never promoted himself yet found himself at the center of history and people's hearts.

Knowing your "Why" has an expiration date as well as a positional element to it. Our

"Why" as a child living with our parents takes on a different hue than when we are 35 and on our own. Being 35 and single our "Why" has different facets to it than when we have a spouse at "35". An employee will have a different "why" than an entrepreneur will, or the boss/supervisor. If you are transitioning from one of these to the next your "Why" will take on different shapes. Celebrate where you were, be grateful for your time on the former plateau and all that you learned there while still looking forward.

The rest you seek is discovered in leaping because of your current "Why". Let me give you four ways to enjoy the leaving of this plateau and leaping to your next.

Remember and reminisce on your gains of where you were. Let you mind and heart celebrate, rather than crying over leaping from here to there.

Enjoy your new now and employee your ability to be "in-Couraged" through your previous successes.

Smile as you face the pressure, predicaments, and perils of this new space through knowing you are where you must be, and these are your new educators not your eliminators.

Trust the process and tabulate the wins more than the losses. It is your responsibility to take charge of your mind and thoughts, you get to decide what hangs on the walls of your thought life. Post the wins in the galley of your thought life and sit and gaze at them often.

Jesus, changed the world, upgraded our lives, and opened the doors of life for all because He rested in His Why!

Oh, yes, Yes You Can!

Now, take a moment and do two things.

1) Call, text, or write someone and let them know how their courage to Leap has inspired you.

2) Send me an email or text me about the Leap you are getting ready to take, so that I can become a person to "In-Courage" you.

Success@MattUpton.net

916.708.8103

JB's Leap Training

Chapter Four

Jackie sat in "Just Right Ground", the coffee shop in downtown Happiville, just north and up the valley road from Goodenoughville. She is waiting on JB her grade school friend, whom she has not seen in many years. A light breeze coming from the east suggest that a change in the weather is on its way. The leaves roll along as if they have no remembrance of their former life, when they were attached to the limb of the tree across the street.

"I wonder how he will look after all these years?" Jackie wondered? The last time she had seen him was the last day of their third grade. Their entire town of Settleville was being relocated due to the new dam. All 1440 occupants, and surrounding families, had been bought out and were given opportunities in the neighboring towns and cities. Her family had moved to the mountains and his family moved just upward and to the north. They had promptly lost contact, yet she thought of him often. She remembered him as a stooped boy who looked as if he was carrying too much weight on his shoulders, his hair always looked as if it needed to be trimmed and combed, his worn-out shoes, and overalls.

The other kids made fun of his appearance, especially his teeth. They protruded forward from his mouth, probably from biting down hard to not speak up when he was bullied. Jackie always saw past all the surface things of JB and because of his heart saw his possibilities. She had never allowed him to get far from her thinking, always wondering how things had turned out for him. She always grieved over the fact that they had lost contact and that she had not stuck up for him every time she saw him being picked on.

Now, almost twenty years later she would have the opportunity to make right what she believed she had done wrong. She would ask him to forgive her for not standing up for him enough and losing contact with him. She had been longing for today for a long time.

She understood that she could not undo all that had happened, yet she had owned her own responsibility, and would do what she could. A man and woman were sitting to the right of her in the corner having a hearty discussion about something she could not make out. Directly across from her were two moms with three children. The kids were well behaved and doing a great job at containing their laughter to their area. By the door a distinguished man (probably) in his early forties sat, typing away on his keyboard, looking completely engaged. Just outside the door was an older couple with their chocolate lab, she is laying with her eyes focused on them as they talk. She has an expression on her face as if she not only understands what they are saying, but as if she is in the conversation as well.

Embracing the ambiance of "Just Right Ground" while listening to the play list that includes songs of strength and courage by Bon Jovi, Rascal Flats, Katy Perry, Carrie Underwood, and many others, she thinks to herself, "There's something about this coffee shop and Happiville that's different", "I wonder what it is?"

As the door opens, a confident well-dressed man walks in as if he owns the place; no, as if he owns everything around him; no, it's as if he connected to everything around him. His smile is like the morning sunlight after a evening and night of rain and his eyes seem to lift anyone he looks at to a higher vision of themselves.

Walking towards Jackie as if he knows her, "Hi, Jackie it is so good to see you after all this time." "I've longed to see you and find out how you are", and "thank you for everything when we were in school together back at Settleville Elementary".

With a perplexed look on her face, Jackie responds, "Well, hi, yet I think you may have me mistaken for someone else? I am not sure that I know you?" his appearance and demeanor were so different than the way she remembered him. "I am JB, Jackie." He answered with a big smile and out stretched hand.

She quickly invited JB to sit down as she is apologizing for not recognizing him. "It happens to me all the time, Jackie, it's all okay, no worries."

They agreed on what they wanted from the coffee bar and began to catch up on the last 20 years of their lives. She was especially interested in the obvious transformation of JB since leaving Settleville. As their coffees, cheese Danish, and blueberry muffin are delivered, Jackie says, "JB, I need to let you know how sorry I am about never sticking up for you back at Settleville Elementary School". Taking a breath she continues, "I was afraid of everyone, and just did not know what to do, I know I do not deserve your forgiveness, yet, if you could I would forever be grateful."

JB, while shaking his head said, "No, no Jackie it is I that came here to make things right between us. I treated you coldly and always kept you at a distance. I am so sorry for the way I made you feel, could you forgive me?" Tears began to roll down Jackie's face and drop onto her blouse, "what? Forgive you for what? You were always so kind to me, and I never stuck up for you, I am the one who was wrong." After a few moments of awkward silence and nibbling on their pastries, the silence was broken by a young lady in a wheelchair with an excited voice, saying, "Hi, JB and thanks for your help the other day." "Ahh, you're welcome, it's always my pleasure to be of service to you, and anytime you need me, just ask. Have a Tremendous Thursday".

Getting back to where they left off, Jackie asked, "tell, me JB, what has brought about all the difference in you since leaving Settleville?"

Taking a sip of his English Breakfast Tea, he looked at her with what seemed like daylight in his eyes and replied "The thought of going to a new school and being treated poorly again, was so difficult. Truth is I wanted to just run away and hide from everything and everyone. I did not know it at the time, I had become filled with bitterness, anger, and resentment over so many things, and it distorted everything."

"I think it's why I did not treat you the way you deserved to be treated. You were always so thoughtful of me and one of the nicest kids at school, yet, I never accepted you and your heart the way I should have."

Another tear begins to roll down Jackie's cheek, "you owe me nothing, it is I who did you wrong and need your forgiveness." With a big grin JB says, "Let's just forgive each other and take it all as a learning time that has made us into the people we are today!" Both shaking their heads in agreement, "and now, tell me the rest of the story that has caused all your transformation."

"As you know my family decided to move here to Happiville, and I was placed into New Perspective School, the only K-12 school in Happiville. The kids were pretty much the same as when we were in school together. The teachers were mostly the same too, yet there was this one lady who worked in the school restaurant."

"She treated me completely different than any adult had ever treated me, she seemed to see me as someone with no flaws and only probabilities. We called her Ms. Patty."

"Ms. Patty became a superhero to me, well actually for many of us. She had a way of making us feel bigger and better about ourselves. She was the first one to ever tell me that I was brilliant."

Taking a bite of his Cheese Danish and a sip or two of his hot tea while he was catching his composure before he could say, "when she first said I was brilliant, I thought she was talking to someone else, or making fun of me. Somewhere along the way she went from telling me I was brilliant to telling me I was just brilliant. Then began telling me that JB meant Just Brilliant."

"I would hurry to school to eat breakfast and could not wait for lunch so that I could see her and see how she looked at me and hear the things she would say to me. Ms. P became a sort of sunlight in my small world of darkness. For nearly four years neither of us missed a day of school."

Someone walked out the door and gestured back at JB, "see you later my friend." With a big wave and a smile towards the man walking out, he begins to tell his story of transformation again, "One day Ms. Patty was not at the school restaurant and I remember being worried that something was wrong and that maybe I would never see her again."

"She seems like an amazing person, JB" replied Jackie. "I wish I would have known her." "Did she come back the next day?" "No, she was away for one more day, she had gone on a little trip with one of her friends." "It was after her return that I asked her what she saw in me that made her think I was brilliant?"

"You see, Jackie my Mom named me Buford, yet because of a communication issue between her, the doctor and my Dad I was named Just Buford." "I did not want to be called my Dad's name and because of how the kids made fun of me being "Just Buford" I began telling everyone my name was JB."

"Somehow, I always saw myself as a less than. I continuously found it hard to accept compliments and praise. It never felt right, after all if I mattered, then I would have had my own name!"

"Yet, Ms. Patty saw something I never did, and that no one else ever saw, taking a breath and whipping a tear from his cheek, he continued. She, said that she had been through a difficult road as well and learned the power of taking a leap to a new way of seeing ourselves. She said that she met a guy that had helped her get a new vision of her life and the lives around her. She believed that working in the school restaurant as the manager was more about helping students see themselves bigger and better than the way in which they have been treated. She understood, that the way people treat us, the way they talk to us, or about us, creates feelings inside of us, that determine how we see ourselves. She promised herself she would always be the kind of person that lifted people up, rather than put them down. She would always do what she could to help others leap to the life that was meant for them.

"I am not sure how long it was after she returned from her trip that I asked her what it was that she learned from the guy that brought about so much change?" "Ahhhhh ... JB it was a simple thing that he told me; he said that I had always been cared for by someone that I could not see, He said that I had been protected and provided for, and that all that had happened was allowed so that I could become the kind of person that helps others take the leap to their bigger and better selves."

He told Ms. Patty that we have two ways to live our lives. The choice is ours, and the choice causes us to see, hear, and feel the world around. He showed her that we can become intoxicated through our bitterness, anger, and resentment, she said he called it "our BAR". This guy also said to her that if we wanted to be free of the intoxicating effect of our BAR we needed to begin raising the BAR rather than going to the BAR.

"What did he mean by going to or raising the BAR?" Jackie asked. She told me that he believed that all of us have our very own special Brilliance and Abilities, that we have to accept and do our best to live in the light of them. He also believed that when we do, we begin to take Responsibility of our lives, rather than let pesky people, pressures, predicaments, and problems have control."

"He showed her that the only way to sober up from our BAR's intoxicating affect is to learn a new way of thinking. Ms. Patty was the first one to suggest to me to make the Leap to a new way of life. She taught me that my BAR was hindering me being my bigger and better self."

Oh, yes, Yes You Can!

It is likely that you have some hinderances that are stopping you from making the Leaps in your life that you know you must make to become that bigger and better person that you are created to be.

Here are five questions to ask yourself that will help you access whether you are being compelled to take a Leap and live based on Leapology® principles.

Question #1

Am I truly fulfilled on this plateau in my life? This answer can only be "Yes" or "No", any other answer is non-committal. Here, now we must Zebra up, be black or white, yes or no. Get real honest with yourself.

Question #2

Does my life make a difference to those around ? Again it is either yes or no. We are here to help others experience fulfillment through how we live, love, and serve.

Question #3

Many times, do you think of the unfair ways people have treated you? If you do, you may be intoxicated from your BAR.

Question #4

In periods of my life when I am asked to try something new, how do I feel? The way you answer this will help you see where the energy of your decision-making process is generating from. This is important, because if you are worried about the opinions of others, or you make decisions based on how someone treated you in your past, the energy level of your soul cannot sustain your Leap.

Question #5

Trusting your ability to make good decisions is paramount, so this question demands total honesty with yourself. "Do I trust my ability to make good decisions? It is impossible to trust others if you cannot trust yourself. The best way to gain trust in yourself is to begin keeping your word with yourself.

Sit down and text me at 916.708.8103 or email me your answers to these five questions. It's time to admit to yourself if you are ready to Leap to your new plateau.

I look forward to assisting you prepare for this next leg of your journey in Leapology®.

Oh, yes, Yes You Can!
Because
You are Brilliant!

You See I told you
Oh, Yes, Yes You Can!

You've just accomplished something that most do not.

You've read through to the half way point ☺

As a reward for you I have created a short video just for you. Just follow this link and enjoy.

Also, text me at 916.708.8103 or email me at Success@MattUpton.net and let me celebrate with you at being part of the elite readers.

You can and will finish this book even though nearly 75% of people will not.

Oh, Yes, Yes You Can!

JB's Leap

Chapter Five

"What I know refer to as my Leap Training, began about two weeks after we returned from spring break of my fourth grade year". "Ms. P had told me about what she had learned from her friend about the BAR just prior to us leaving school for break"

JB smiles and waves at a Mom leaving Just Right Ground and says, "I could not stop thinking of what she told me about me being Brilliant and that my BAR was holding me back." "I had to know what needed to be done to sober up and make the Leap to the best version on me!"

The best version of ourselves comes into existence as we live within our now and face tomorrow with confidence. Many of us are like JB living in the fog of regret and resentment of our past. We cannot live here and in the past at the same time.

The regret and resentment of events of the past weigh us down, causing us to be incapable of making our leaps. Laying aside these weights that so easily hinder us, is paramount! While we are dwelling on our past, we begin to believe six lies.

Lie #1

That because of what happened to us we cannot have what's best. This lie creates a repetitive loop of regret causing us to miss out on our best. This loop becomes proof to us that we are correct in that we deserve to live a smaller version of ourselves.

Lie #2

That somehow we caused what happened to us and therefore deserve all the mistreatment that comes to us.

Lie #3

That because of what happened and all the disappointment I've caused my family, there's no way I can be loved or liked. This lie also creates another repetitive loop. A loop of rejection, which we view as something we deserve.

Lie #4

That because of what happened, no one will ever want me to be in their life. They see us as damaged, scared, and difficult, so they keep their distance. When people become cold and detach themselves from us, we accept it as our lot in life.

Lie #5

That because of what happened to us, I cannot trust people. I was hurt by someone that I was supposed to be able to trust and they hurt me, so I will never trust again.

Lie #6

That because of what happened I am how I am, and people must accept my harshness or not have me in their lives. After all I cannot change what happened and therefore I cannot change me.

These six lies become weights that hold us back. They stop us from making any real effort towards leaping forward. We live our lives always knowing things were supposed to be different yet can never be different because of what happened in our past.

There is nothing that can be done to make what's truly wrong right. Yet, because terrible unjust things have happened to us, does not mean that we cannot leap to be the best version of ourselves. In the grandstands around you are multitudes who are cheering for you to leap, they know you can, because they have.

These witnesses in the grandstands suffered unjust treatment, violations from people they believed they could trust, and misfortune. Each them learned the same thing that Ms. P did and sobered up from their intoxication from their own BAR.

The cheers of those in the grandstands having nothing to do with having faith or a positive attitude. They are cheering from a position of fact, because they leaped, and they know you can.

Making their leap involved four practices. These practices are the same for everyone who lives their life based on Leapology®. Along with Ms. P, her friend, and JB, you will need to practice each of these four steps to make you leap to your bigger and better self.

Practice #1

Forgive as a lifestyle. Forgiveness is less about the person who harmed you, or the circumstance that hurt us, and more about us. True forgiveness is releasing ourselves from being the jury, judge, and jailer over the painful event of our past.

This is a lifelong practice that must be woven into your daily journey. Regularly express forgiveness and release towards those who hurt you, this grants you the ability to take responsibility for your life.

Living in unforgiveness becomes our justification to remain in our smaller lives. We convince ourselves that because we were hurt or mistreated we can play small and be fulfilled. Yet, never discover satisfaction, only a life of complaining.

The longer we have lived in our self-created "Smallville" of our lives, the greater the intoxication you are experiencing from your BAR. You will need to practice forgiveness often. It may be several times a day, it may be several times an hour, or it may be ever several times a minute at first.

Practice #2

Align yourself with those that are moving forward in their lives. There is a unique power that is experienced as we align ourselves with those that are industrious with their Time, Talent, and Treasures.

Though it is true we cannot spend all of our time with people who are moving forward in their lives, we can spend less time with those that are not. Each of us only have 1440 minutes given to us in a day. The way we invest those minutes determines our Leap distance and stamina.

There are four kinds of relationships we must maintain to live a life of fulfilment.

Relationship #1

Keep a relationship with the best version of yourself, learn how to visit with your best self. Our minds are mini time machines that transport us to the past, the future, and the present.

This transporting happens as the result of a thought that occurs due to some external stimulus. A song plays on the radio, a smell roams across our nose, a sight lingers in our eyes and poof we are in another place. Within this time machine called our minds, exist three versions of us.

The vision is what we were, what we are, and what we could be. Spend time with the best version of your future self, the one who has overcome. The one who has confidence in your present self. It is this future version of you that compels you to be courageous and Leap forward.

Relationship #2

Develop relationships with those that have Leaped forward in their lives and are reaping the rewards of their courage. These people accept everything as a learning and equipping event that is preparing them to be the best version of themselves.

Learn to listen to them, ask deep questions, look at their Leap zones. Yours will not be the same as theirs, yet the practices and principles they used to Leap will be nearly identical to what you will use.

Their courageous spirit will serve as a spring board for you as you stand at the edge of your comfort zone. Their courageousness will become "In-Couragement" to you.

Relationship #3

Maintain a relationship with those that are at the same space in their journey as you. This relationship will be spent in three ways; just being together enjoying life. No agenda is the first segment of time spent, the second is compelling each other to get up and get with it, and the last, and least amount of time, will be used in visiting over the anguish through the journey.

As you use the moments in the relationship as suggested it will be transformed from an expense to an investment.

Relationship #4

Construct bridges and gates for those that are running their race to their various Leap Zones, yet have not covered as much ground as you. Leave road signs of direction and warning.

This is accomplished through three consistent exercises. The first is record your wins and learnings along your journey, live what you've learned and wait for them to ask you the "how" questions, and last celebrate their progress along their life's journey. Let them know that you see and are encouraged by them.

Celebrating their progress towards the best version of themselves will do more to open the gate of connection than any other thing you can do. No one cares how much you know, until they know how much you care. The most powerful sense of being cared for happens in moments spent together, and words of affirmation.

Practice #3

Capture your setback viewing them as setups. This practice creates courage through any obstacle that presents itself along your journey to your next leap.

There's only one way to gain the courage to grab setbacks and turn them into the building material of your leap zone, it's facing problems, pressures, and persistent pesky pain and moving through them despite the fear.

The manner in which you think of, and speak of the setbacks from problems, pressures, and persistent pesky pain determine whether they become setups or cages for you to remain captive in them.

Practice #4

Transfer the unexplainable, unpredictable, and unreasonable events into the hands of the one who provides for us, protects us, and propels us forward in our journey to be our best selves, and to experience fulfillment

This transference is impossible if much of our 1440 minutes are spent in regret and reviewing what happened with yourself or with others. It is a difficult habit to change, yet it can be accomplished. Creating a habit of transference, is not for the weak at heart.

Here are four exercises you can use that will increase your soul's capacity to transfer.

1) Begin to ask yourself what you learned about yourself and life through the unexplainable, unpredictable, and unreasonable events.

2) Live by Grandma's motto "if you have nothing nice to say, say nothing at all" to yourself or another.

3) Rather than lamenting over the unexplainable, unpredictable, and unreasonable events locate the launch points to the "better way".

4) Shrink the time you spend listening to doom, gloom, and blame reports from family, friends, foes, and the news.

As you stand there gazing across the crevice between this plateau and the one over there, remember you are provided for, protected, and propelled to Leap.

The first step, that first level of letting go and leaping is the most difficult. Your soul will speak, rather blaring at you to stay put, yet you cannot, you sense your better self is calling you "Leap over here, You've got this!".

In the movie "The Last Crusade", the second in a series of films by Steven Spielberg about a man named Indiana Jones, there is a scene in the movie in which Jones must traverse a great crevasse or his Dad will die, and the crusade will be over.

Indiana Jones comes to the opening, looks at his little book, and says "it's impossible, no one can jump this far", "it's a leap of faith". Knowing there's not much time, he steps out though everything he could see, hear, and feel told him stay put.

Stepping out into what appears to be thin air, his foot lands firmly on an invisible bridge. A bridge that is camouflaged from the sight of anyone who has never been there before. The only way forward is to step out on what seems to be a foolish move to be able to discover the fact of the provision and protection that had been provided by someone he has not met.

After safely making the journey from one side to the other, he stoops and picks up dirt and tosses it out on the bridge. As Indiana Jones marked his journey so must we. For we know not who will come this way, nor do we know whether we will need to pass this way again.

Transforming a Leap of faith into a Step, into a fact, must be experienced through participation. It cannot become fact by mustering up my emotion, reading about it, or hearing about it. It can only be done through taking a Leap forward.

As you stand there contemplating your leap, let me know where you are. Text me at 916.708.8103 or send me an email to Success@MattUpton.net and let me know you are ready to Leap On.

I want to "In-Courage" you and you let go of where you are and begin to embrace your new Plateau of Fulfillment.

To Leap or Not Leap

Chapter Six

September 14, 1989 just two days after the birth of his last child, a little girl, he began a new career. It was in a new city, a new boss, and a new level of responsibility.

He had spent 12 years in his previous position and was experiencing success on every level. A great staff, plush new office, spectacular group of people to serve; so why did he leave?

It is easy to make decisions when it's a clear choice between good and bad. All of us can choose amid the obvious best choice, yet what happens when we are caught between what's best and what's good?

When we choose what's good rather than the best, we shortchange ourselves, those we serve, and we change our future.

When the call to leap to your new plateau comes it usually comes with a conflict of conscience. Many times, others will do what they can to talk you out of the leap you are considering.

They mean well. They love you and cannot bear to see you experience a setback, or the agony of defeat. Yes, there are times your family and friends become foes to your call to be your best self. The challenge is to give heed to the call, while honoring those who have loved and supported you.

This call to leap is mysterious as well as majestic. It is our future self-calling back to our current self. The part of us that has made the leap and has made the discoveries of success is compelling us to make the leap. It urges us to come on over, your life is here, you can make it. We already made it.

Our former self and all its failures, hurts, and disappointments is suggesting to us to stay where we are. It reminds us of all the pain we've experienced from attempting to leap in the past. Our former selves are well versed on everything that went wrong, and therefore can go wrong. It tells us to, move away from the edge and settle down, and put our Leap away.

Your past self will bring up the following 15 emotions that are capable of limiting you

from living a life through the principles of
Leapology®. They come from deep within us
and are in our own voice. Sometimes they
emanate from the hearts of those that love
us. Yet, if it is a true calling to take the leap,
it will only serve as limitations and cause us
to take up residence in Smallville.

If we stay in Smallville for long, we will
become smaller and smaller in our own eyes.
How can we live our life as everyone else,
when we are designed different than
everyone else? Everyone is called to take a
Leap to grow into the unique person they are
meant to be. Oh, Yes, Yes You can!

The fifteen Limiting statements that serve as
anchors and eventually create smaller
versions of who we are meant to be, have a
grand purpose. They serve as the proof that

we are at the edge of a new leap in our journey to our best self.

Let's take a look at all fifteen of these statements. For some they limit them and to others serve as the very building materials that are used to launch them to their next plateau. The leapers perspective determines whether they will stay or take the leap.

Limiting Statement #1

"*No Way!*" We hear from within us this statement as we look at the evidence of our past, our short-comings, and our failures. We disqualify ourselves before we even give it a shot.

Transforming this statement into building material happens as we say, "No Way, I cannot do this based on failures, short-comings, and my past. I can only do this by trusting that I am protected, provided for, and propelled forward by the unseen, as well as with my GPS."

Your "G.P.S." is the part of your makeup that represents your **G**ifts from birth. These were installed in you while being formed in your mother's womb. These are closely aligned with your **P**assions, which draw you towards you likes and away from those activities you do not enjoy. Then there is your very own **S**uper power. This is what draws people towards you, gives you the clarity to solve issues that others cannot, and causes you to be attracted at times to "save the day".

Limiting Statement #2

"I Can't!" The strength of this statement is it is partially true. You've never done this before and it's a leap into an unknown area of life, so you say to yourself "I can't". In some ways these first two statements serve as the moving crew to pack us up and relocate us to our own Smallville version.

Transforming this statement into building material happens as we choose to focus on two thoughts. The first is to recall all the leaps you've made in the past that you believed you could not do and did it anyway. Then say to yourself (out loud if needed) I cannot take this Leap alone. I will make it with the assurance of the one calling me to make the leap, and the confidence of the successful leaps I've already made.

Limiting Statement #3

"It's Impossible." This statement will show up through your own soul's voice as well as in the voices of loved ones. To others, this leap of yours is impossible, yet to you it is your destiny.

Transforming this statement into leaping material involves an act of your own will. You must take charge of your thinking and turn its focus toward the possibilities of success. This is done in two simultaneous movements of thought.

Change "It's Impossible" to "It's I'm Possible" and at the same time look towards where you are going and see the possibilities.

Limiting Statement #4

"Maybe I'll do it later?" This statement masquerades before us in many forms. Its most consistent characteristic is that of complaining and believing someone needs to do something about the issue. This statement often partners with statement #2 and tells us that we can't because we are not qualified.

Transforming this statement into building materials happens as we involve ourselves in learning and activity. Once we gain a little experience we will gain more confidence.

Limiting Statement #5

"I'm too Old" This statement is fortified through comparing ourselves to people who do not have our experience and wisdom. All such comparisons will serve to limit the possibilities that are just beyond this leap.

Here is a short list of those that transformed this limiting statement into the building material of their leap into greater success. They did this through focusing on what they must do and their previous leap successes.

✓ President Ronald Regan was elected to his first term in public office at the age of 55. Nothing on his resume of previous leaps indicated that he would go on to be a two-term president of the United States of America.

✓ Jack Cover, though you may not recognize his name, you've seen or maybe experience his leap to success that happened when he was 50 years old. He had spent most of his career within the aerospace industry, yet through a desire to incapacitate assailments without killing them, he began his new company and gained a patent for his design four years later. At the age of 88 when he stepped over into eternity, his invention called the Taser was in use in 45 countries around the world.

✓ Anna Mary Robertson Moses, is
another name you may not know.
Yet if you were an American Folk
Art buff, you'd know who she is by
her most popular title of,
"Grandma Moses". At the age of
76 years old as a result of painful
arthritis she was forced to give up
embroidery and try something
new. She took a leap and for the
first time in her life picked up a
paint brush and used it to paint
her first canvas painting. That
was in the mid 1930's, and she
would go on to live another 25
years and she lived to see her
paints that she originally sold for
$3.00 be re-purchased for upwards
of $10,000.00.

✓ Tim and Nina Zagat left their careers in the law world to influence people in choosing the restaurant they would eat at while traveling for business or pleasure. They began a report that we know as "The Zagat Report" which was purchased by google in 2011 for a mere $151 million.

✓ Harland Sanders whom we know as "Colonel Sanders" began his chicken empire at the age of 65. In 1952 when Interstate 75 opened and began taking people away from his restaurant and hotel a few miles away, he refused to allow it to break him. He began to research how to prefect his blend of spices for the best fried chicken.

Once he was satisfied, he began touring the United Sates and selling franchises that would be called Kentucky Fried Chicken Restaurants. In 1964 when he sold his business for $2 million there were over 900 franchises nationwide.

✓ Laura Ingalls Wilder wrote and published her first book at the age of 65. She went on to write and publish one of the most beloved children's books series, that later became a tv series entitled "Little house of the Prairie"

Age has nothing to do with your ability to make the leap. It has everything to do with your commitment to losing your "quit" and focusing on "there's gotta be a better way" focus.

Limiting Statement #6

"I have no idea how?" Imagine if you would have bought into this statement when you were first propped up against the wall and coaxed to walk? Or if you would have walked away from getting on that two-wheel bicycle? Maybe when the opportunity for your first real kiss presented itself?

You would still be living your life without having ever experienced the immense pleasure of a kiss. You would still be riding that old red tricycle. We learn how while in the process of leaping to new experiences.

My scars I received from learning how to ride now serve as trophies of not giving up because of the pain of falling. The look of shock in her eyes after my first kiss became the desire to learn how to be better.

The setbacks that come through transforming this statement into the material to leap into "I now know how", become the catalyst to confidence and courage.

There are some great hitters in the game of baseball that just see the ball bigger, which enables then to hit them more often. Yet, most have to stand in the batter's box, let the pitcher throw a 99 mile per hour curve ball at them, and maybe get hit a few times before he can learn how to hit the ball.

Life is the same for most of us, we must fail our way forward. You and I are the people who have learned what it means to go through the "trial and learn" process of leaping forward.

The scars we gain through this process become the very springboard that propels us to our new plateau of life.

Get out there, step to the edge, and leap with your fear, it will stay behind as you soar on through what you learn.

Limiting Statement #7

"What about my family?" This partners really well with Limiting

Statement #8 "What would my parents think?" Both of these limiting statements are a cleaver disguise of "I am just not ready, nor do I believe I have the ability."

In most cases your family wants your greatest success. In those few times they do not, it could be because of their own Limiting Statements they are making to themselves about themselves. The only help you can give them is your own audacious success.

There are four reasons why they cannot express their support of your plans to take the leap. They will speak from their fear and anxiety of your willingness to take the leap.

1) They are dependent on you either emotionally or financially. Either will hinder them from being able to freely give you "In-Couragement" to Leap on.

2) Their past failures are being projected onto you and your future. Their great love for you will not allow them to support you leaping into (what they view as) harm's way.

3) They are intoxicated through their frequent trips to their own BAR, their unresolved Bitterness, Anger, and Resentment. It is impossible for them to see, hear, and feel your reality while they are inebriated from their own BAR.

4) They are assaulted by their own conscience as you speak of and prepare for your leap. They are reminded of a time they stood where you now stand, and they stepped back. Regret has been their reward. Now, you are reminding them of when they moved back to Smallville and accepted a smaller version of themselves.

While they want to become your cheerleader, they cannot at the peril of their own life of excuses.

Through love, honor, and respect look at where they are now and ask yourself, "Do I want to be there later in my life's journey?" If your answer is a resounding "NO!!!", then Leap on.

Limiting Statement #8

"What would my parents think?"
(Re-Read Limiting Statement #7)

Limiting Statement #9

"It's never been done." It is untold how many problems still exist because of this pesky limiting statement! Imagine if people like Wilbur and Orville Wright, Thomas Edison, Alexander Graham Bell, Susan B. Anthony, Claudette Colvin, Lewis Latimer, Marie Van Brittan Brown, and Booker T. Washington would have succumbed to this statement. We would not experience light by electricity, fly in a plane, make phone calls, live as free people, and so on, and so on.

The reason it has not been done yet, is because you have not done it. Your capacity to complain about it is proof that you play a part in the solving of it. This can only happen as you Leap On!

Limiting Statement #10

"I do not have the time" This statement is such a cushy and debilitating excuse to stay comfortable. Since the dawn of time every human being has had the exact same amount of time to accomplish their task. Regardless of technological advancements, we have the same amount of time in each day that our ancestors had. The difference is the

mastery of task management and focus our on those tasks.

The 18th century farmer and the 20th century scientist are granted the same 1440 minutes in a day. The ability to transform this Limiting Statement into the building materials to leap is discovered in conquering task management rather than being subdued by focusing on time management. It is impossible to manage time. Yet, it is possible to manage our task within our allotted 1440 minutes.

The secret to task management is discovered in two paradigm shifts. The first one is to recognize that less is more. We must begin to let go of the many things we do and focus on fewer task. The second is allowing others to pick up the task we are not gifted for, don't have passion for, are not equipped to accomplish. This causes us to see the need of working in teams with people who have different gifts and equipping than we do.

I use a system I call Take Six® to accomplish "less is more". It was created through my failure to manage time along with the futility of long list of things to do. My long list created within me a picture of my consistent failure. I discovered that at the close of everyday my list looked as though I had not made any progress, which caused me to give up on making list.

Now just about every week I use a few minutes on my Setup Sunday and write out all the task that need to be completed this week. Then I group the task together that naturally go together and complement each other. After this, I move just six of those tasks over to Magnificent Monday's list of tasks. As I complete each task, I mark them off as completed. Then that night a few hours before resting for the next day, I move six more task over to the next day. This is done every night for six nights. I regularly leave one day with no task to accomplish.

Though it is true I accomplish much more than just six task a day, I only bring over six per day. This allows room for the unexpected issues to be successfully handled, while at the same time feeds my need to experience daily accomplishments. This system also gives me the capacity to have the courage to let my "yes be yes" and my "no be no" If you would like to try this system out, you can download a copy of the form I use at www.mattupton.net/free-resources/takesix . Before you download these pages, make an agreement with yourself that you will use it for a minimum of 4 weeks. After you've fulfilled your promise to yourself, make the needed changes in the system that will best suit you.

Limiting Statement #11

"I do not have enough money."

Money is attracted to solutions and to

those people who are committed to serve others. Very few leapers began their journey with enough money for the entire journey. It was their commitment to solve the problem and serve for the welfare of others, that opened the gates and lit the way for financial resources to find them.

Every great parent I know, began their journey as a parent with less money than they needed to give their children a better future than they had. It was their unending sense of duty to their children that caused them to do whatever needed to be done to have the financial resources needed to create a future of fulfillment for their kids.

Recognizing that you are both protected and provided for along with your heart to Serve creates the avenue of resources. It also lights the way to you and your solutions. Begin your leap while you reframe your lack of focus on the vast supply that is available to every industrious leaper.

Limiting Statement #12

"Nobody believes in me." Waiting for everyone to believe in you before you leap finds its strength in our lack of confidence in ourselves. Their lack of belief in you is because they cannot see, hear, and feel what you do in your soul.

Our lack of confidence grows under the black lamp of doing nothing. Turning on the light of activity produces the confidence we yearn for. The family and friends we want to believe in us will as we leap to our plateau, and live within our success. They will tell the story of our success and it will cause them to move towards their own leap zones.

Limiting Statement #13

"I do not have enough knowledge."
Everyone that leaped from one plateau to their new one, did it with a lack of knowledge. We cannot know everything about the new plateau until after leaping there. Even after being there and transforming it into a new comfort zone, we will not know everything about it.

While in our frame of humanity we exist in a space of not knowing everything. It is within this space that we leap through the faith that we are provided for, protected, and propelled to live in the unknown. We are meant to thrive in the unknown.

Learn as much as you can by taking advantage of all the resources within your grasp. Yet, it is in your leaping that the greatest levels of knowledge will be illuminated to you. This new knowledge we become energizing for you.

Limiting Statement #14

"It will always be like this, nothing can be done to change it." Many use this statement to justify their lifestyle of doing nothing to make things better. They just moan and groan about how

things are, and they blame everyone else for their condition. These people who have set up residence in the this limiting statement, wait for someone else to solve their problems while at the same time believe they did nothing to cause their situation.

You are incapable of living a fulfilled life in this space because you've heard your future self-calling to you. You've seen within your soul the better and bigger version of yourself. There is no entity, no government, no person except you that can bring about your life of fulfillment, and that only happens through your leap.

Limiting Statement #15

"It will be too difficult." Yes, it will be difficult. Leap on! This statement anesthetizes your soul's ability to live from the power of possibility thinking. To transform this limiting statement into a launching platform we must practice the following three things:

1) Accept the fact that difficulty is part of living and moving forward.

2) Redefine difficulty as a signal that you are moving in the right direction.

3) Recognize that difficulty endured gives birth to fulfillment.

Now that you have disarmed the power of these fifteen limiting statements and transformed them into material for your leap zone, send me a text or give me a call at 916.708.8103, or send me an email of what your M.A.P. is beginning to look like. I look forward to partnering with you as you make your leap.

The Leapologist®

And

Their Trust

Chapter Seven

"We would like to have you become part of our team" he announced, and he followed that up with an offer that was truly amazing. Becoming part of their team would come with multiple financial allowances, vacation, incentives, medical insurance, and various other benefits, along with a base salary of close to twice what I was currently making.

The offer seemed like a call to make a leap in that direction, yet there was a nagging yellow light flashing deep within my soul.

How do we know when an opportunity is an opportunity, or just another distraction from where we are designed to be? One question would reveal the answer. How do we discover the one question that will illuminate the Leap Zone? This illumination happens through learning to trust five things and living in seven daily practices. We will discuss the seven daily practices of Leapology® in chapter eight.

The Five Trust of Leapology®

Trust your Gut

When your souls yellow light is flashing, pay attention to it. It is there to advise you to use caution. Just like at an intersection when the yellow light comes on, it is suggesting we slow down and proceed with caution.

Some see the yellow light and change its purpose to say to us, step on the gas pedal and get through this intersection quickly. Each and every time this is done, three potential consequences loom in front of us.

1) Colliding with another automobile or person while going through the intersection that we were meant to stop at.

2) Receiving a moving violation for going through an intersection that we were supposed to stop at and wait for the green light.

3) Successfully making it through the intersection with no collision or moving violation. Yet, within this success comes a dulling of our ability to trust the warning system in our own soul.

Remain loyal to your own gut warnings, they are there to keep you in a journey forward to your own fulfillment. There are three messages that your Gut wants to communicate to you.

> Gaining ground is accomplished through thoughtful Leaps that enable you to Serve in a greater manor.
>
> Unify yourself with those activities that fulfill you rather than make you happy or increase your status.
>
> Triangulate this moment in light of who you are, who you Serve, and the responsibilities you've already agreed to.

Refuse to leave a trail of your puke

Every Leaper from time to time gets ill in the space they are in and puke a bit. Yet, to let your puke be the reason to Leap will hinder your leap and actually cause you to land in an unintended space.

When a person gets sick and gets nauseated to the point of puking, the great concern is that they will become dehydrated. Even mild dehydration adversely affects mental performance and increases feelings of tiredness. Mental functions affected include memory, attention, concentration and reaction time. Common complications associated with dehydration also include low blood pressure, weakness, dizziness and increased risk of falls.

What happens to us in the physical realm also happens to us in our soul when we puke for extended amounts of time. When we spend a large chunk of our time doing the following four things, we are dehydrating our soul.

P Pausing and pointing to what's wrong, dark, and the injustices of the past or present; the ails and troubled areas of our culture; and how you've been victimized by authority figures or people. When this occupies much of our social media time, thought time, and verbal time it is puking from your soul.

U Uncharitable to those who have differing world views from you and not resist in taking about them, and their incorrect vision of the world, causes an unstoppable stream of puke coming you both verbally and in written form.

K Keeping the conversation in your head and heart, and with others, focused on the incorrectness of those that differ from you or have wronged you. Also it is nearly impossible for you to connect with someone outside your thought community, you cannot leap forward.

E Engaging in tearing down the views and the people who differ from your world view. Rarely do you engage in becoming the change you want; most of your rhetoric is about what's wrong and little is said about what's right.

The cure for a person who is physically dehydrated is rehydrate through drinking water. When you and I have become dehydrated in our soul (mind, will, and emotions) we need to rehydrate as well.

Rehydrating our soul involves two practices. The first is to involve ourselves in solutions rather that pointing at problems, pressures, and pesky people. While connecting ourselves to activities that lean toward solutions, get to know the people who inhabit the opposing view from yours. We do this through learning to listen to learn rather than being a critic.

Here are six daily exercises that will increase our ability to listen.

1st Daily Practice to increase our ability to listen:

> Log out of all conversations within yourself before logging into the conversation with someone of an opposing world view.

2nd Daily Practice to increase our ability to listen:

> **I**nvest with your eyes and ears in the one speaking as if they have a treasure within their words specifically for you.

3rd Daily Practice to increase our ability to listen:

> **S**erve them through our total presence in this conversation.

4th Daily Practice to increase our ability to listen:

> **T**riangulate the conversation to be about them, You, and the Us you can become.

5th Daily Practice to increase our ability to listen:

> **E**ngage in thought filled question that focus on "Us" and what you

do not understand about how they came to their world view.

6th Daily Practice to increase our ability to listen:

Negotiate and navigate the possibilities rather than the problems, pressures, and pesky people.

These six daily practices will require a courageous and confident setting aside of your need to be right along with the heart of a learner. As you practice each of these daily practices you will increase your ability to listen and discover that life will lighten up.

Unify your commitments to match your G.P.S.

As we've lived and thrived on our current plateau we made many commitments. These commitments were to enable us to care for our families, fulfill our responsibilities, and sustain our life fulfillment.

Prior to taking the leap to the next plateau, make certain that you have fulfilled all your commitments, or that the leap will enable you to fulfill them.

Always leap towards fulfillment. Fulfillment of your commitments, or as a means to fulfill your GPS, either in your family life, your volunteer life, or in your career life, needs to be pondered.

Speak well of all people

My Grandmother used to say, "Grandson Matt, when you have nothing positive to say, say nothing at all." In truth I have no recollection of how often she would say this, I just know she modeled it and it stuck with me.

The basis of accomplishing this is to stand firm on a foundation of "all of us are created equal". There are no favorites in the heart of the creative handiwork of God. Each of us are protected, provided for, and propelled forward equally. Opportunity knocks on our soul's door based two things.

1) Our GPS; Gifts, Passions, and Superpower. Remember our gifts are within us from conception and our passions are in alignment with those gifts.

2) Our response and reaction to our B.A.R. Yes, we can get through being intoxicated at our B.A.R. "Bitterness,

Anger, and Resentments" create passions that flow in conflict with our gifts. This will create situation where we leap into mirages.

Our G.P.S. is constructed through our D.N.A. because we are "Designed Naturally to Achieve" a fulfilling life. Every one of us are placed in the correct time period, proper surroundings, right levels of ease and difficult situations, and people to bring us to a fulfilled life. Approaching the five Trust of Leapology® with a sense of gratefulness will produce an ability to be possibility focused.

Translate difficulties and dilemma's as delivery agents of treasured gifts:

The T.D.S. syndrome seeks to corrupt every organization, both for profit and nonprofit endeavors, neighborhoods, cities, counties, states, the nation, and world. Yet, its main prey is you.

This debilitating syndrome cannot be held in your hand, seen under a microscope, or spotted through a telescope. It is breathed into our soul through our attitude's, words, and actions.

It is the way we respond to **T**rouble, **D**isappointments, and **S**tress. When we respond through the intoxication caused from our own B.A.R. then we actually weaken our soul's immune system to ward off the T.D.S. syndrome. The level and amount of time we spend thinking, talking, and puking about T.D.S. determines its capacity to grow and control us.

To increase our soul's autoimmune system, we must consistently do two things. The first is remove and destroy our critics hat and then become a learner. The time we spend as a critic of Trouble, Disappointment, and Stress is time we are connected to its power source. While we are being connected to its power source we are being infiltrated by its destructive energy.

Eventually we are unable to see its power of control over our soul. We actually begin to believe this is how life is meant to be lived. When our own B.S. is being controlled by the intoxication of Bitterness, Anger, and Resentment we drift from our DNA and our GPS gets confused.

Recovering from this intoxication and rebooting our GPS happens through taking the multi vitamin called celebrate. The nine soul fortifying ingredients in the Celebrate vitamin.

1. Consistently live up to your own word.
2. Eliminate your own and stop attending Puke Sessions
3. Liberate yourself to truly listen
4. Emulate your high expectations of others

5. Bring your best self and serve everyday

6. Retell the good stories of life

7. Adjust your attitude

8. Triangulate conversations to Us solutions

9. Elevate other people

We will spend more time in chapter nine discussing this powerful and life changing vitamin.

The one question that illuminated the difference between an offer of fulfillment of my design, or a distraction became clear because of the trust in my gut. That one question was, "Will I be able to speak and present as I am now, when I become your employee?"

His answer became a lamp post that illuminated how I should respond. He promptly informed me that there would not be time to conduct the trainings, do the Transformational Coaching, and keynote presentations while serving as an employee of his organization.

With confidence and courage, I expressed my gratitude for the offer and turned it down.

As you increase your foundation of trust in yourself and create your leap zone, Text me at 916.708.8103 or send me an email to Success@MattUpton.net and allow me to celebrate your increased foundation of trust as you prepare to Leap to your next plateau.

As a fellow Leapologist® you give me vast amounts of courage. Thank you for permitting me to Leap alongside you.

Daily Practices

Of

Leapology®

"hot cup of coffee, cheeseburger, and fries"

Chapter Eight

Walking into the Diner that afternoon for a cheeseburger, fries, and a hot coffee with no idea that he was walking into one of the most fulfilling Leap opportunities of his life.

Alvis never shrunk from his life's responsibilities. His wife of 20 plus years succumbed to lung cancer. As a young widower for just two years, placed him on another a course that no one would choose. To everyone in that diner that day it looked <u>like a gentleman having lunch, yet for Alvis it</u>

was a Leap Zone in to one of the greatest fulfilments of his life.

He and his Francis (as he often referred to her) had one son whom they loved with all their hearts. Elgin was the apple of his parents' eyes, they did everything they could to arrange life with the greatest of possibilities for their one and only child.

When His lovely Francis became ill, they began to spend more time on the Northern edge of the central coast of California in Santa Cruz. They loved the beach and the board walk. It was here that she could breathe much easier and they imagined a time where they might live and raise their son near the ocean.

Yet, fate would not allow them to build the life they imagined. Francis passed away. Alvis and Elgin's lives took dramatic twist and turns. After the honoring of her life in their church she was buried in the Tulare city cemetery and both Alvis and Elgin attempted to return to life as they had known it.

The grief of losing his wife and raising their son without a Mom, proved to be much more difficult than he anticipated. He poured himself into his work in an attempt to fulfill his responsibilities as a Father. This placed him away from the house quite a bit leaving his son at home alone a lot.

Alvis knew he needed something more for him and his son. He wanted his son to have a <u>Mom and family</u> to come home to after school.

The decision was made that Elgin would move into his Uncles home and become a daily part of their family.

Yet, Alvis never saw this a permanent situation, he just was not sure how to create a family atmosphere in their home. The entire time they were separated, He prayed to the one that he knew had protected, provided, and propelled them forward, to give him the answers to this terrible situation. It was difficult on both Elgin and His Daddy during their separation. Elgin suffered a double loss during that time, the loss of his Mom and now his Dad.

Though they saw each other many evenings for supper and on Sunday's for church. They normally spent the entire day together on Sunday, eating, talking, playing croquet, laughing, listening to the radio, and long walks together in silence.

Alvis never lost hope that they would one day be back together under the same roof and at the same kitchen table. He just did not know when or how?

Both were forced to take a leap they no one would have raised their hands and chose. There are some leaps we find ourselves in the midst of that do not come through an act of our will or anyone else, it is because of a series of circumstances that seem to fall into the category of unfair and unjust.

When we read through the life of someone, we can begin to see daily practices that form their life perspective. I got to spend a lot of time towards the conclusion of Alvis's life.

Listening to him talk and share his life's story with anyone that would take the time to sit and read him, I saw seven pillars or practices that characterized his life.

It is likely that if you would have had asked him to name the practices of his life that gave him the incredible life he had, he would have articulated the following seven. I am sure he would have made it much simpler.

My time with this humble and honorable man gave me the privilege to read through his life's journey. When we read through a life we are doing four things.

First: **R**ecalling the steps of their life's decisions and circumstances.

Second: **E**ngaging in the events of their life, both the good and not so good, the difficult and easy choices, the light and heavy circumstances along their life's course.

Third: **A**nalyzing and accepting all the outcomes of a life lived.

Fourth: **D**etermine the value of those circumstances in light of their destiny.

The following is my read on one of the greatest men I've ever had the honor to know. These are the Seven Daily Practices of my Grandfather.

1. Stay True to Yourself

Through all the circumstances he was dealt, he always did his best to remain loyal and true to the man he wanted to be. A man of faith, love, and loyalty to his family. Every decision he made came through this grid of Love, Loyalty, and Family. He remained True to Himself even through the grim hallways of his Alzheimer's.

2. Serve while putting People before possessions

He saw as the highest calling of his life was being a husband, Dad, and Grandpa. Though they lived on modest means, he always had a few coins for a ride on the Giant Dipper Roller Coaster at the Santa Cruz Beach and Boardwalk with his grandkids. As far as I know he gave near all of us our first ride on that old-time roller coaster.

I remember one time we were in line together and he had allowed a family to go in front of us. I supposed he was just being kind to them, so they could all sit together. He bent down and whispered in my ear, "life is like a roller coaster ride, to enjoy it to its fullest get in the front seat of the first car and raise your arms in the air through the entire ride."

3. Set some of your financial resources aside to keep

Grandpa believed that some of all he earned was his to keep. This belief caused him to do two things with each and every paycheck. He gave 10% to his church in honor of God and 10% in the savings for the rainy days and nights that he knew would come.

He lived off the closely managed 80% left over. When he stepped over to the other side to begin a new life, he left no debts.

4. Savor good books, especially the Good Book

The first "grown up" book I ever read was given to me by my grandmother and grandpa. Every time I visited their home, there were books on the end table they were in the process of reading and always in the stack (usually at the top) was their Bible. It was a nightly and morning ritual that he would spend some time reading from what he sometimes referred to as the "Good Book", his Bible.

5. Stand with people of wisdom, integrity, and triumphs

He loved to talk of people of great wisdom, integrity, and triumphs. Many times, when I would visit with him in his younger days while they lived in Tipton, California he would take me to see the accomplishments of people he admired.

We had many conversations of King David, Daniel, Theodore Roosevelt, John F Kennedy, and pastors whom he believed had accomplished great task.

6. Sit in silence and pray, seek, and ask big questions

When I read through my own life, Grandpa may be the first one I ever seen who would just sit in silence. In truth I thought that was because he was Grandpa, and to me very old and that's what old people did. Yet, I did not have a clue, that many times as he sat in silence he was asking big questions and expecting big answers, seeking the heart of the one whom he believed protected, provided, and propelled him forward. He was praying, watching, and waiting.

Through this lifelong daily practice, he gained wisdom beyond his formal education, love with no borders, and miraculous provisions that showed up right at the precise moment of need.

7. Start your day the evening before

One night while spending the night with my grandparents I asked him if he had any regrets in his life. Without hesitation he answered that he went through some difficult, disappointing, and disastrous times, yet no regrets. He went on to say that it was through all those that he had learned to appreciate the good times and love people deeper.

I remember asking him how did this? He said he believed that we are supposed to begin our day the night before. "What?" I asked. He told me that he always ended that day with an expression of gratitude for the day he had just finished, they people he met, the circumstances he managed through and asked for wisdom and courage to make through another day in honor of himself and the one whom he believed cared for him like no one ever had.

That day in (what I remember being called_ the "Burger Queen Diner" in Tulare, California Alvis Burner, my grandpa experienced the invitation to another Leap Zone. He was served by a polite, confident, and attentive lady named Inez Jackson. While Grandpa sat at the counter opening up his newspaper and began to read, she asked from the other side of his paper, "Sir what may I get you?"

As he peered over his newspaper, deep within his soul he sensed the appearing of his next Leap Zone in his life of Leapology®. He once told me that she was the most beautiful woman he had ever seen. Which he said (almost) every time they would see each other to his last days of life on this side.

He answered in a slow gentlemen manner, "I would like a hot cup of coffee, cheeseburger, and fries Ma'am" and I am sure he had that handsome grin of his across his face. Years later while he was recounting this story of their first meeting, I asked him what he did? He promptly told me that he went back the next day for another "hot cup of coffee, cheeseburger, and fries".

They were married in August 1962 in Tulare, California and spent their first night together in Bakersfield. After spending their honeymoon in Disneyland, they came home and picked up Elgin and brought him home to his new family. Now Elgin had brother, five sisters, and a lady who would grow in to becoming his Mom.

Being prepared for your Leap Zones through these Seven Leapology® Practices will prepare you for the unknown.

Leap On

Oh, Yes, Yes You Can!

Do me a favor my fellow Leapologist, send me a text 916.708.8103 or an email Success@MattUpton.net and let me know how you've been Provided, Protected, and Propelled forward as you look back and read your life's journey to your current plateau.

The vitamins
of the
Leapologist®

"Leapologist, leap on"
Chapter Nine

August 2011, I had the honor of meeting three remarkable Leapologist. We were brought together through our involvement in a nine-month intensive training course for aspiring speakers who were looking towards building a career in the public speaking world.

Part of the training placed us in smaller groups designed to help each of us put together 5 minutes speeches. Theses speeches were to be presented before the entire class and instructors. Afterwards we would be critiqued to increase our abilities to convey our messages, connect to our audience, and create moments that would be captured.

There was a total of five of us in our small group. One was a remarkably successful woman who was the president of her multimillion-dollar company, myself, and these three Leapologist. The remarkable thing about them was that each of them were knocking on the door of their 7th decade of living and loving life.

Gary had spent most of his career as a tax man. He believed there was still much for him to do in helping others live their fullest through the financial management skills he acquired. It was his goal to help others make wise money choices that would enable their money to go farther and accomplish more.

Gerry (pronounced Jerry), had achieved wild success through his salesmanship. He could sell about anything, and when his contemporaries were coasting into the twilight of their lives, he wanted to help others learn the science of sales. He proposed to accomplish this through writing books and speaking from the stage.

Paulette was in the midst of retiring from her speech therapist career for a local school district. Yet she believed that her life's story needed to be in the hearts and minds of others. She believed that her experiences could help change the world of those that she could tell her story and truths to.

Their energy and vitality inspired me. They were tireless in the quest to serve those they believed their experience would become an antidote to the poison of limited thinking. They seemed to know that what they had to share would become an elixir for the "success thirsty" they wanted to serve.

We saw each other about twice a month for about a year, and then once a month for close to three years. They never tired in their pursuit to serve their community. They were always ready to make the adjustments in their writing skills, stage presence, and speaking business practices to allow them to serve.

I always wondered where they got their unending supply of stamina to leap forward. They never seemed discouraged, disappointed, or distracted because of pressures, problems, or pesky people. Looking back over those years, I came to believe they had a special diet that fed their soul.

This diet made their soul healthy. Which in turn gave them physical health, energy, creativity, and to celebrate their lives with an ability to leap from one plateau to the next. They did this with an incredible sense of ease. I envied and admired each of them. They caused me to want to have the same diet for my soul. It is clear to me they each of them regularly enhanced their lives and soul through eight essential vitamins.

Vitamin #1

Consistently live up to your own word:

When they say they will be there to do a certain thing at a certain time, they are there. Never once did I see them fail at fulfilling their commitments.

Along with living up to their word, they always let others do their task as they see fit. They waited to be invited in to a coaching relationship with others. Though each of them has years of wisdom and experience and would have done things differently, never have I witnessed them putting someone down because of their difference.

This diet supplement has allowed them to remain focused on their serve without being distracted through how someone else is doing something.

Vitamin #2

Eliminated their own or attending Puke Sessions:

Through their decades of working alongside many different kinds of people, and attitudes, they learned that expressing their puke or allowing someone to puke on them was a waste of precious time and effort.

There are four elements of a puke session:

Pausing and pointing to what's wrong, dark, the injustices of the past or present, the ails and troubled areas of our culture, and how you've been victimized by authority figures or people. When this occupies much of our social media time, thought time, and verbal time it is puking from your soul.

Un-charitableness towards those who have differing world views of you and cannot resist talking about them and their incorrect vision of the world. You have an unstoppable stream of puke coming from you both verbally and in written form.

Keep the conversation that is in your head, or heart, and with others focused on the incorrectness of those that differ from you or have wronged you. It is near impossible for you to connect with someone outside your thought community.

Engage is tearing down the views and the people who differ from your world view. Rarely do you engage in becoming the change you want, most of your rhetoric is about what's wrong. Little is said about what's right or where your version of right exist.

Vitamin #3

Liberated themselves to truly listen to others:

There were many times I watched them take this vitamin. It is a hard vitamin to swallow when you have a large ego. Our ego will cause us to gag while attempting to ingest this pill. Yet, time after time all three of them modeled passionate listening in front of me and with me. They mirrored the six aspects of how give a powerful listen, while at the same time never condemning me for my inability to fully accept this vitamin in my soul.

Here are the six elements of the vitamin of Listen:

> Log out of all conversations within yourself before logging into the conversation with anyone.

> Invest with your eyes and ears in the one speaking as if within their words, there's a treasure for you.

> Serve them through our total presence in the conversation.

Triangulate the conversation to be about them, you, and the us you can become together.

Engage in thought filled question that focus on "Us" and what you do not understand about how they came to their world view.

Negotiate and navigate the possibilities rather than the problems, pressures, and pesky people.

Vitamin #4

Emulated the high expectations they had of others:

Paulette, Gerry, and Gary had experienced limiting biases from people, they were never going to be characterized like that to others.

This commitment to speak well of others as well as live "free of limits" was a driving force in their lives. They seemed to know that we were watching them to discovered how to live the way they were, thus they made choices that would be the example for us.

This triad of wisdom emulated their expectations of people in five ways.

1) When the spoke of others, they always spoke in an upward manor of their character.

2) When asked to do something there were times I heard them say "no" I do not have time to accomplish this on time, or they would say "someone else is more qualified than me".

3) They regularly managed their task, so they would redeem their minutes of each day. They spent their 1440 minutes a day doing the things that only they could do and left the rest to others.

4) They were constant learners. All three of them regularly sat near the front of the class and took notes. Through the notes they took they analyzed and adjusted their steps to enable them to be better as they gave their serve.

5) When they offended someone, as soon as they became aware of the offense, they did what they could to made it right.

Vitamin #5

Bring your best self and serve everyday:

This was a motto they lived by. It did not matter if they were part of a committee, the president of the organization, in the midst of honoring their platform, or being with their families, they always brought their best Serve.

They brought their best serve through four concepts that became a four-step dance for them.

Dance Step 1

Be someone who finishes what you started

Dance Step 2

Enlarge the lives of those you serve

Dance Step 3

Serve for the benefit of the organization, people, and their success

Dance Step 4

Trust the process with the knowledge that we are Protected, Provided for, and Propelled forward

Vitamin #6

Retell the good stories of life:

Each of them faced dark, depressing, and disappointing times through their lives. Yet, at every telling of these events they painted them with an artist ability, bringing out the good within each story.

Through listening to them tell their stories, I saw the art of bringing out the good. They did this through seeing their lives as art and that they were the ones painting on the canvas of their life.

They accomplished their art through three practices in all they did.

Acceptance of pressure, problems, and pesky people as gifts to enlighten them to be their best self and live a better way.

Responsibility is ours to take and grow through.

Transferring their wisdom was more important than recalling the pain and injustices of their lives.

Vitamin #7

Adjusted their own attitude:

They recognized their attitude was the only attitude they could adjust. They understood that any time spent in attempting to change someone's attitude is wasted time. Life is to short and moves to fast, why waste it on efforts that may never happen.

It is best to take charge of our own attitude rather than attempting to manipulate or control another person's.

Vitamin #8

Triangulate conversations to Us type solutions:

This always surfaced in our discussions. They regularly asked questions like, "What can we do to make this better for everyone?" or "How will this decision affect all of us?". This served as a reminder to me that it's not about me, they, or them, it's about us. It is in discovering and accepting our differences that US solutions surface and we become stronger.

Vitamin #9

Elevated other people every opportunity they had:

They did this through regularly giving a smile to those they were listening to, or having a conversation with. They consistently ran people up rather than down when talking about them. They did this in their presence and when they were not around.

This triad of wisdom and stature repeatedly elevated me. They always made me feel as though I was better than I actually was, had more insight than I did, and caused me to live up to their good opinion of me. I know they did this in both in my presence and in my absence.

Paulette, Gerry, and Gary live their lives based on the principles of Leapology®. I am forever in their debt for how they "incouraged" me to leap into service and then sustained me through their words and presence. When I was not sure where a leap zone existed, they either were there to point to it, or they had marked it out so that I could locate it.

These three are into their seventieth year of their life and are still leaping from one comfort zone to discomfort. Each time they make a leap they learn more and celebrate all they've learned, all the ways they've served others, and how they remain fulfilled. They are living proof that pursuing fulfillment is the best leap of all. I believe they would say that chasing happiness is exhausting, yet capturing fulfillment brings happiness.

Leap On My Friend

My fellow Leapologist, I want to celebrate with you your art of fulfilling your life's mission. Send me a text to 916.708.8103 or an email to Success@MattUpton.net and let me share your success in displaying your art of Leapology®.

Caution, there's No Going Back

"The former plateau is no longer there"
Chapter Ten

To the entire world March 5, 1955 was a normal spring day. Yet for 15-year-old Claudette, it is the day that she will always remember as the day she was forced leap into a new life. She will inspire a movement, and she would never be the same.

Claudette entered a short story in a writing contest through her school. The winner of the contest will have their story printed in the local newspaper. She did not let her family know about the contest, because she wanted to no one in her family has ever entered a writing contest.

Walking into the family kitchen for breakfast the aroma of southern breakfast filled the entire home. Three of the most important women in her life, her Mom, Auntie, and Grandmother were busy making lunches and serving breakfast to their loved ones. Claudette ate fast, so she could get to the bus stop and to school to find out if she won the contest.

Yesterday while leaving school her teacher stopped her in the hall to tell her how much the committee enjoyed reading her paper. This served to heighten her anticipation of the outcome. Her family would be so proud of her if she won.

Kissing grandmother good bye and wishing Auntie a good day, and a quick "I love you"

Mom, and young Claudette is out the door on her way to her leap zone that would change everything.

Today's leap would forever change her life and cause the world she knew to disappear. Every Leap Zone comes with both a destructive attribute and a creative one. Once we leap from this present plateau to the next, the old can never be lived in as it once was. From now on everything changes.

After the ride to school on the city bus she exited her bus saying. "I will see you this afternoon" to the bus driver. Her teacher was standing and greeting all the students as they walked in and found their desk. "Claudette, after roll call, come see me at my desk. I have something to talk with you about."

Each student answered "Here" and finally roll call was complete and she could go up to the front and find out what her teacher wanted to tell her. Making her way to the front and doing her best to conceal her excitement about the writing contest.

Handing Claudette her paper back, the teacher commented on how wonderful her story was and how all the committee believed it was the best. With a growing smile, Claudette asked, "did I win, will I get to be published in the newspaper?"

Her teacher went on to explain that they would not be able to publish the story in the local newspaper. "No, Claudette your paper will not be printed in the newspaper, they just do not print articles from people like you."

The silence and sadness hung in the air like rolling fog pushing it way across the hill side, engulfing and hiding everything in its way. Her teacher attempted to sooth her as she rolled up her paper into a small cylinder. She began to whisper, "it's just not right, something must change, it's just not right."

The rest of her school day meandered along like any other school day. The final bell rang, students gathered their belongings, and headed outside, and to the busses that would deliver them back home to their families. As she stepped on the bus that day, to her it was just as it had always been, yet the events of the day had transformed the bus into a leap zone.

There are two kinds of Leap Zones: the ones you create through your G.P.S. "Gifts, Passions, and Superpowers". They create spaces that cause you to leap towards the next phrase of our life.

Then there are the Leap Zones that appear in front of us which we had little to do to create them. These appear because of a gathering of circumstances out of our control. They are created through someone else's decisions, and or a set of circumstances create them.

Today, March 5th, 1955 would be such a day for Claudette. As she was walking to the rear of the bus where she always sat, in the area she and those like her sat. Two seats from the division of the front and rear of the bus, she saw an empty seat, looked at it for a moment, and sat down in it muttering "it's just not right, something needs to change."

A few stops later a lady who wanted to sit in (what she always viewed as her place) asked and then demanded Claudette to move from there and go to the back of the bus where she belonged.

Claudette remained seated while whispering "it's not right, something needs to change". She was eventually dragged off the bus by two policeman and taken to jail. Later that night a lady by the name of Rosa brought the bail money to get her out of the jail cell and take her home.

Six months later on December 1, 1955 Rosa Parks sat on the bus in (maybe) the same seat. She became the starting point of what we now call the Civil Rights movement. What most of us do not know is that 15-year-old Claudette Colvin is the one who became the lightening rod of courage that caused Rosa to sit in the seat that brought a nation to its Leap Zone for equality.

When Claudette took her Leap into history in early March 1955, she had no idea that the world she once lived in would disappear, making it impossible to go back.

Every Leap zone brings destruction and creation. Just as certain as the earth spinning and creating the allusion that the sun both sets and rises, it is certain that both the unexpected and expected Leap Zones will appear.

The turmoil that is caused through taking your leap is twofold, the new plateau comes with new pressures, problems, and pesky people. It also involves the challenge of many of your comfort zones while you build your new life on your new plateau.

The other factor that creates turmoil is there's no way to leap back to the life you once had. Your former plateau is no longer the same the moment you leap. The security and comfort you experienced there is gone. You can never go back to it and experience exactly what you had prior to your leap.

Regardless of your reason or motivation to leap, there's no going back to what once existed.

Here are seven aerobic exercises that will create within you the soul stamina, capability, and capacity to live and thrive on your new plateau.

Negotiate your new plateau while honoring all that has been, and what you learned in your old plateau. Do not look back with a desire to return, what you remember and reminisce over no longer exist. Except in your imagination.

Engage in your new life with confidence and courage, knowing that you are provided, protected, and propelled forward. Also, others have made this sort of a leap prior to you, they are cheering for you. Listen to their cheers of "In-Couragement", feed off of it.

Those who have never taken this sort of leap, have no ability to give direction. Accept their cheers for you, nothing else.

Work will not be simple in your new life. It will be grueling at times. There will be difficult, disappointing, and stressful times ahead of you. Accept them as supplemental vitamins for your soul, that will build your stamina. As you work through each dilemma your strength will grow as well as your confidence.

Liberate yourself to live within your superpowers. Become aggressive with saying "no" to those things that with distract or weight you down from the task that serve you best. Get enough rest each day, the work will wait for you. Spend replenishing time with people who are energy givers, stay away from those energy takers as much as you can. Eat balanced meals, you will need your health.

Investigate your new life as if it has buried treasure for you. The treasure it has for you will not make itself known to you or deliver itself to your door step. Though it is there it must be sought. Once found you will need your strength to uncover it and make it yours.

Face the storms before they arrive as while they are pounding on you. Prepare in advance for the coming storm though you cannot see it right now. Recognize the universal truth that there's always a storm coming. Then when it hits, face it, and gather all your resources and live through it. You will be wiser as a result of the storm. It comes to bring you a gift. You must remain loyal to your New Life to gain its precious gift.

Evaluate every circumstance, every pressure, every problem, every pesky person episode with the knowledge that all things work together for good for those who life is characterized by the principles of Leapology®.

Once in a while when I was a boy, I would wander into the kitchen as Mom was creating her delicious meals. I would watch as she put a dash of this, and a pinch of that, then a smidge of that with great wonder. Sometimes I would ask "Mom why are you putting that in there?" she would answer because all of it together will make what we are having for supper much better.

Your New Life is the same way, each Pesky Person episode, problem, and pressure by themselves will never feel good nor bring the gift they have the capacity to deliver. Yet, as we accept them as the ingredients that are designed to create a life of fulfillment, they become less painful. Mom knew how long to cook the dish and at what temperature for it to come out wonderful and nutritious.

The one who protects, provides, and propels you forwards knows the length and duration you need to make you the best version of you.

As you make the move to your leap zone and take your leap, you will face multiple dilemmas, disappointments, pressures, problems, and pesky people episodes. These are yours as a gift, not a curse. They are meant to increase you, not destroy you. They are designed to be creative not destructive for you.

The way I as a Leapologist get their gifts is to remember the five principles of the ruby. I carry a ruby in my right front pocket all the time, have one on my desk, and in my mobile office (my vehicle).

Now that you've come to the end of the book, I have a gift for you. If you will call/text me at 916.708.8103 or email me at Success@MattUpton.net and let me know that you've completed this book and give me your address I want to send to you a ruby.

The five life principles within the ruby are life enhancing. Take the ruby and hold it in the palm of your left hand.

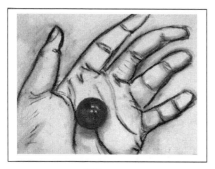

Now with the ruby in the palm of your left hand, pull your pointer finger down over the ruby, and **R**emember who genuinely loves, appreciates, and believes the best of you. Now do something vastly different with your middle finger than most of us use it for, and pull it down over your ruby, **U**ncover the gift of learning that's in this difficult situation that you are facing. Next pull your finger that's between your middle finger and your little finger and **B**e the Bigger and Better self that those who genuinely love you know are. Bring your little finger down to join the other three fingers over your ruby and if you're anything like me, saying I will be the bigger and better person is easier said than done, and **Y**ield to your commitment yourself to be this person. Finish by pulling your thumb in making a fist over your ruby and grip it with gratefulness. Your ability to Leap with gratefulness will give you the capacity, courage, and confidence to live a life based on the principles of Leapology®.

It has been my pleasure and honor to spend this time with you while you read this book. I am your friend, your cheer leader, and fellow Leapologist®. When I can do anything for you, just ask.

Oh, Yes, Yes You Can!

Leap On

Oh Yes, Yes You Can!

Additional Tools to Aid in your Leap:

One free two-hour TCS "Transformational Coaching Session", Call 916.708.8103 or email me at Success@MattUpton.net to calendar your two hours.

Download the following:

Choose Your Day poster
www.mattupton.net/free-resources/posters/choose-your-day/

Take Six Task Management System
www.mattupton.net/free-resources/takesix/

No Puke Zone Poster
www.mattupton.net/free-resources/posters/no-puke-zone-poster/

Grant a TAAT Poster
www.mattupton.net/free-resources/posters/taat-poster-2/

60 Gemstones
www.mattupton.net/free-resources/60-gemstones-i-discovered-along-this-journey/

Connect with me on Facebook
www.facebook.com/USpeakingofSuccess/

Leap On my Fellow Leapologist®

Leap On

Made in the USA
Columbia, SC
09 April 2019